I Might Be Wrong, but I'm Not

VOLUME 2

This is the property of the
The Great Freddy Velez

Copyright © 2024 by The Great Freddy Velez

All rights reserved. No part of this publication may be reproduced, distributed or transmitted in any form or by any means, including photocopying, recording, or other electronic or mechanical methods, without the prior written permission of the publisher, except in the case of brief quotations embodied in critical reviews and certain other noncommercial uses permitted by copyright law. For permission requests, write to the publisher, addressed "Attention: Permissions Coordinator," at the address below.

The Great Freddy Velez / Author's Tranquility Press
3900 N Commerce Dr. Suite 300 #1255
Atlanta, GA 30344, USA
www.authorstranquilitypress.com

Ordering Information:
Quantity sales. Special discounts are available on quantity purchases by corporations, associations, and others. For details, contact the "Special Sales Department" at the address above.

I Might Be Wrong, but I'm Not/ The Great Freddy Velez
Paperback: 978-1-966088-04-2
eBook: 978-1-965463-74-1

I Might Be Wrong, but I'm Not

I believe that if things aren't going your way today, tomorrow is another day, and another, and another, and another. Sometimes patience pays off.

Believe.

I believe that if doing something nice makes you feel good. Just do it. No compensation needed.

Hallelujah!

I believe that being a good human being adds years to your life.

Halle, are you listening?

I believe when you come face-to-face with a challenge and give it all you got, you will triumph.

Believe.

I believe that you should do what you want to do as long as you do it well. Doing good feels good. Ask my wife.

Good god!

I believe that if you let family members know that you are there when they need you, they will call. You are that rock that they need.

God bless.

I believe trust is just one phone call away. You want a relationship, one phone call away. Need a friend, one phone call away. Need food, one phone call away. You just need to talk to somebody, just one phone call away. Call, you will feel better.

The Great Freddy Velez

I believe that if you really want to be satisfied and don't care what people will say, get the twenty-four-inch Philly cheesesteak with all the works. Good God Almighty.

I believe Tiger Woods could be playing better golf if you put hair around a little hole. If you put hair on the two holes, he probably could put both balls in.

Strategy, my man.

I believe that if billionaires gave more to the people that don't have anything to eat instead of millions to the worst of art museums, this would be a better America.

I believe that if you work, make good money, and spend it just on yourself, you are not a good human being. By helping your fellow men, you aren't a lot of friends instead of enemies.

Looking good is not the same as feeling good.

God bless.

I believe when the going gets tough, the tough runs away and hides.

So much for toughness

I believe in the American dream, it is a dream that for some of us, is to linger on for a long time and then some.

Believe.

I believe that I'm a victim of the Halle Berry curse.

Thank you, Lord!

I believe the reason things happen is because they had to happen. You can't hide when it is your turn to have something happened to you. You can prevent things from happening for a short while. But if it is in the Lord's book, it was going to happen.

You can take that to the bank.

Praise the Lord!

I believe the reason I command respect is because I impress the opposition.

I believe in all honesty that my two-year-old granddaughter is a better artist than Pablo Picasso.

Now show me the money.

I believe you cannot resolve a dispute without an effective discussion.

I believe that a woman that looks so passionate is actually more trouble than you have time for or thing for.

I believe that choosing the right girl can double what you have now.

Believe.

My time in this world is precious. That is why I spend a lot of time with family and friends.

Time is precious.

The Great Freddy Velez

I believe that if you ask questions and observe, eventually, you will understand.

I believe that I am a little blunt sometimes, but that is part of my charm.

Good God.

I believe, and I don't know why, but I really enjoy watching people improve and grow and get ahead. Why? I don't know. But it is like a great pleasure to my insides.

Go figure.

I believe that when you least expect it, he will find something that you were looking for three months ago. It was always there. You just didn't look there.

Go figure.

I believe I am a little stubborn, but I know how to deal with it.

Shut up.

I believe I want answers, and I will persist until I get them. Holly, are you listening? Big daddy is waiting for his answer.

You go, girl!

I believe that when a person pays his or her dues, doors will open. Another level of power and privileges and responsibilities and desires, and oh god, I'm burning up.

Good lord!

I believe that when two siblings are playing checkers, one of them has to be Black. Get it?

Black.

I believe the less a man or woman knows about that person they like, the nicer it seems. Then poof.

Go figure.

I believe it is important to foster a pet. That is why I got married. My wife is my pet.

Good God.

I believe my pet (my wife) makes me feel secure, loved, and overweight.

Lord, have mercy.

I believe anybody can be a reality star. All you need is no talent, the ability to curse, and act stupid.

Believe.

I believe that in order to learn self-discipline, you have to have a good hold of your temptations.

I believe that sometimes the best way to help is by doing nothing.

Go figure.

I believe that when you try to be perfect, that's when disaster strikes.

The Great Freddy Velez

I believe there is no life without principles. I know because in school I had a principal that got my life together.

And how good, Lord.

I believe that in order to live life to the fullest, you need patience, and a little money will help.

I believe that people that go to jail for crimes that are not outrageous should be punished by listening to music. Like soundscapes, Lawrence Welk's easy listening, classical masterpieces in Christmas music year-round.

Lord, this is a punishment.

I believe this world needs a few good men. Well, I'm here. We just need the other few.

I believe everything I get in this world, I owe to three people. Mostly to the Lord will allow my mother to fool around with my father and out came this hunk of a man.

Thank you, Lord.

I believe in all honesty that if you see a three-hundred-pound man doing the hundred-yard in under ten seconds is because he's being chased by some woman's husband.

Praise the Lord.

I believe deep in my heart that beauty comes in all shapes and sizes, colors, nationalities, and religions.

I know.

I Might Be Wrong, but I'm Not

I believe that just because you are the oldest person around your group of friends does it mean you are the oldest mentally.

Just a number.

I believe that if you wait for the big ship to come in, you are going to wait for something that may never show up.

I believe you cannot assume that your friends can do anything for you but instead will you might do for them.

I believe if you enter into a friendship cautiously or even shy, you may have more in common than you think.

Cautiously.

I believe that just because your feelings were hurt doesn't give you the right to hurt that person back.

Talk.

I believe that if you feel uncomfortable, it is time to investigate the situation. It could be just you.

Adapt to your surroundings.

I believe that if you look at the patterns of events around you, you are not surprised. You can predict the outcome.

Act surprised.

I believe people get excited when teaching others about what they know because it makes them feel like they are on the same page. This is when you realize that you are now in a competition.

The Great Freddy Velez

Go figure.

I believe that if you believe that a person's integrity is questionable, it is because it is. The gut never fails.

Gut feelings.

I believe in living a great life; that means accepting Halle Berry into the family and continue moving forward.

Good God, hallelujah!

I believe Halle Berry doesn't realize that we have more in common than she realizes. Diabetes.

Go figure

I believe that if you live life with full participation, this will help your way of thinking in business decisions.

Commit.

I believe, and I mean this from the bottom of my heart, people have no idea what they really want when they show anger, or is that their appeal?

Go figure.

I believe, and I really believe this, you can make the first move, and you will be respected.

Believe.

I believe if you want to move with the times, just stay in line.

I will ou take initiative you will have a lot of followers. Family always needs a leader.

You are it.

I believe if you take initiative, make sure you are true to yourself. Otherwise, you are just out to gain favors.

I believe that if you think it is funny, it is because it is. There's nothing wrong with laughing at yourself.

I believe that if you really want to heal, forget past heartaches. You have the ability to start new.

What is happening now is what counts.

Believe in the Lord.

I believe that letting go of the painful past has made me a better human being and a more positive person.

I believe just when I didn't think I could love my wife any more than I do now, she goes and cooks my favorite food.

Lord, have mercy.

I believe external things don't define a person. It is what is inside that person that defines them.

I believe that at 350 pounds, I'm bigger than my thoughts and feelings. Go figure.

I believe an organized person knows what they want and what's important.

The Great Freddy Velez

I believe some fool doctor says that the average person blinks ten thousand times a day. Is this how we spend our taxes?

Good grief.

I believe in all honesty that if a woman asks a man out, it is because she wants his body, and if he is a doctor, lawyer, or CEO of some company, she wants his bank account.

You go, girl.

I believe if a man asks a woman out, all he is interested in is her body.

Praise the Lord.

I believe that after the second mixed drink or third beer, you should stop drinking. After that, all women begin to look like Halle Berry, Beyoncé, Eva Mendes, and J.Lo. Before you know it, you wake up thinking that you reach the mountaintop, but it turns out, you are on top of a four-hundred-pound woman.

Oh, God!

I believe deep in my heart that President Obama is our third Black president. Abe Lincoln and Bill Clinton preceded him.

I believe, and this I know for a fact, President Obama is our first mulatto president.

I believe that white rice goes with anything. Yes, I do.

I believe the last time that was beautiful, it was on a two-year-old baby. After that, you're obese.

I Might Be Wrong, but I'm Not

Who knew,

I believe a four-hundred-pound woman cannot see her privates.

Good lord!

I believe a four-hundred-pound man needs a mirror to see his privates.

No kidding.

I believe when you see people really happy at seven in the morning, it is because they have sex last night.

Whoa, baby!

I believe, will I know, that the Rockefellers play monopoly with real money.

I believe that at five feet ten and 350 pounds, Denzel Washington, Brad Pitt, or George Clooney don't have anything over me. I believe they call a man like me, a sex object.

Good God.

I believe everybody should take their fifteen minutes of fame and try to make as much money as possible. After all, it will only last fifteen minutes.

Good grief.

I believe that love with the lights on or love in the dark can still get you in trouble.

I believe.

The Great Freddy Velez

I believe my dog feels so bad for me when he saw my paycheck that he decided to leave the house. He sends me a note telling me that he has gained ten pounds since he left. He said homelessness is not really that bad. He said he found a nice b——. A Saint Bernard with no puppies. He said not bad for a poodle. He said thanks for everything, and he signed with his left paw.

Now that's gratitude.

I believe that two fried eggs over white rice are a gourmet meal when you don't have anything else.

Oh yeah, baby!

I believe that I don't believe in sharing your good fortune with the next guy. I am not about to share my wife with anybody or, for that matter, not Halle Berry either.

No sirree, Bob.

I believe you call a girl with a big butt "Hercule-a——."

I believe you call a girl with no butt "No Butt."

Sounds fitting.

I believe if love is a many-splendored thing, then why am I not getting any? Is it because after so many years married they laid you off? Or is the spice not there anymore?

Go figure.

I believe you call a man with a big muscled body Hercules. A woman with a big butt, hercula——or Oprah Winfrey.

I believe that any man can lose their life with an overdose of love. Women are more dangerous than a pitbull with rabies.

Take that to the bank.

I believe TTTTB means take that to the bank, but what about if you don't have anything, then you take it to the TTTTWF. Take that to the welfare office.

I believe that women who look mean look mean because their panties are too tight.

I believe that men who look mean look mean because they haven't got any in a while.

Take that to the bank.

I believe these men that look mean look at me because they haven't got any in a while, then my boss hasn't gotten any in years. That's a mean son of a female dog. Take that dog to the pound please or have them fixed.

I believe, and this is a fact, that when a person is going to be put on death row, it is because they got to choose your last meal. Why can't they choose your last lay and die happy?

Praise the Lord!

I believe with all this writing I've been doing I haven't gotten laid in a while.

Take that to the bank.

I believe that I raised my kids in the Catholic religion. Now some are Jehovah's Witnesses, Pentecostal, and Seventh-day something. Well, I did my job right. They all believe in You, Lord. Born-again Christians.

Hallelujah!

I believe that getting lei in the morning is a good thing. Nice way to start the day, and they are nice flowers.

Gotcha!

I believe that in Hawaii before you pick up your luggage, you get lei. Now that's how you start a vacation. Who said there is no happiness in this world?

I believe people that are in prison for long sentences should be able to join the infantry division in the armed forces and send overseas to defend our country. Those that make it back and parole.

Those that don't get released early, at least
they tried to do good for a change.

I believe you don't have much of a life if there is no controversy in it.

Go figure.

I believe if you have too much controversy in your life, you have no life.

Oh, brother!

I believe the saying goes, you only got one life to live. Then why do they keep talking about reincarnation? Please make up your minds. I need to know so I won't mess up.

I believe that if you mess up in your first lifetime, there's no reincarnation for you.

Case closed.

I believe I would like to ask the rabbi, priest, pastor, clergy, brother, or minister if a person or people that are born or died on 666 or six 666 go to heaven or the highway.

I believe 666 is 18/3 and the age when you become an adult.

Do the math.

I believe more time is wasted thinking about doing something worthwhile than actually doing something worthwhile.

I believe the pen is mightier than the sword, but the tongue is mightier than the pain.

Take that to the bank.

I believe peanut butter and jelly sandwiches are a lobster dinner to the poor or homeless person.

I believe that if you give a millionaire peanut butter and jelly sandwich for dinner, that person would probably put out a contract on your ass.

Ungrateful.

I believe Puerto Ricans are in a class by themselves. They or we have light skin, dark skin, white skin, Indian skin, people, all born and raised on an island.

Damn, we are good!

The Great Freddy Velez

I believe that when the going gets good, everybody wants in. When the going gets bad, the rich walk away.

I believe I will know I'm not rich. I know I'm not poor, and I know I'm not middle class—that's a fact. But I do know that I am a survivor, a good one at that.

I believe the Lord gave me this body because He didn't want my wife to worry about other women.

Thank the Lord.

I believe if you want the day to start good, have a Puerto Rican breakfast. That's whatever you find available, rice, beans, soup, eggs, pork chop, and steak. We are not choosy about her breakfast. We believe that's where happiness starts—a full stomach.

Yeah, homey!

I believe that I have never met anyone who doesn't crave positive reinforcement. If you haven't, time to speak up. Be heard.

Nothing to lose.

I believe that women should not bring a baby into this world just to hold on to their boyfriend.

Jacka——!

I believe that not all your seeds will turn out perfect. There is always one that thinks limes and lemons are the same. No matter what, they are still your seed and you should love them as they are.

No matter what, love.

I believe that life insurance and lifetime warranty ends on the same day. Somebody gets your life insurance. Nobody wants the warranty. Under these circumstances, I refuse to die.

Gotta go anyway.

I believe that being slick is a job that requires a lot of maneuvering.

I believe that if you are from a third-world country and you have leftovers, this is called a miracle.

Believe it or not.

I believe that if you have a cement floor and you are a senior citizen but you hear floorboards creaking, think, that could be your knees.

Good heavens!

I believe that all arguments on the Super Bowl Sunday should be delayed until after the game.

Postpone all arguments about kids, work, politics, religion until Monday.

I believe that (male children/grandchildren) just because you shave your mustache, this makes you a man. Try again. You will always be my baby boy or boys.

I believe that every parent is different. Some parents use creativity, others blackmail, others reverse psychology, others, cookies, and milk just to get a child to take a bath.

It works.

The Great Freddy Velez

I believe that if you want to have kids or grandkids with superpowers, start with Oreos and work your way up.

Good parenting.

I believe that there is a proper way to address the elderly. Manners, attention, awareness to express yourself is a start.

Respect.

I believe that if you take your time knowing people, it brings better results and more success using this approach.

Try it. You'll like it.

I believe that if you are going to give, give little by little. It is more appreciated, and it keeps people interested.

Give.

I believe that if you have a thankless job, you are doing it for personal reasons and the food it puts on the table.

Yes.

I believe that if you are going to repeat past mistakes, make sure they were good ones.

I believe that music plays a big part in what you will do today. Music of any kind will put you in the mood.

Believe it.

I Might Be Wrong, but I'm Not

I believe that if you want attention, you should break a policeman's car window. It will get attention.

Believe it.

I believe my feelings are what make me irresistible.

Go figure.

I believe that if you have hope and optimism, you have made it.

Made in the shade.

I believe peanut butter and jelly is a meal. Bring on the milk.

I believe some people are better by the thoughts of their future. What future?

Live now.

I believe that if you rely on people to do as they're told, you are one hell of a person.

I believe that if you want it to happen, you have to make it happen. Jump at the opportunity.

Jacka———!

I believe that with my thoughts and fantasies, I could go to jail. Halle Berry, stay away! You hear me?

Oh, lordie, lordie, lordie.

The Great Freddy Velez

I believe that the Lord gave us life but not to do wrong. It's a gift that we should not take for granted.

Do the right thing.

I believe life is a gift that you just keep unwrapping and find amazing things.

I believe that with a little more organization, you can bring whatever you are doing to a workable end.

Hallelujah!

I believe a lot of people take too much for granted about their own talent. They need to look at past family members to recognize our connection.

I believe that the person telling you how it is done is because they respect you and count on you.

I believe that if you think nobody has the right to tell you what to do, then you are an original jackass. Nobody was born knowing everything.

Jacka——!

I believe that the people trying to put things into perspective for you are the people that love you.

Jacka——!

I believe there is a cure for every ailment in the world—it's called positive thinking, or garlic.

I believe if you are given the opportunity to show people what you do best, jump at the opportunity and show off.

It opens doors.

I believe that the only people that don't need rules or those that don't play sports or board games and people who are not married.

I believe that sometimes long-distance communication can come in handy.

I believe that everybody should have a backup plan in anything that they want to accomplish or be in.

I believe you should use your imagination to consider all points of view like what can go wrong or what will work.

I believe that if you provide great service, you will be married for a long time.

Good God Almighty!

I believe that if you give 100 percent in whatever you are doing, people will notice even if you don't.

I believe that if you get emotional when you are making love, you are a wimp.

Sissy!

I believe that you make a lot of growing up when you make mistakes.

Believe it or not.

The Great Freddy Velez

I believe that if you work hard and play hard, you have earned everything you have.

I believe you should not let your nerves dictate your life. Go for what you want and insist.

I believe a lot of times that a young person can inspire you into doing the right thing.

Believe it or not.

I believe—well, I know—it feels great to get out of the gutter and start over.

I believe it is nice to smell the roses if you are not allergic to them.

Some of us have beauty to celebrate while others can find it not even looking in the mirror.

Damn!

I believe children are wonderful to have, even if they drive you up the wall sometimes.

Believe it.

I believe that if you were going through hard times and your head is just barely above water, don't give up. The man upstairs will take care of it. He is just testing you. Have faith. He will provide.

Believe.

I believe that if everything in your house is falling apart, then it is time to move. Get a new place.

Jacka——!

I believe in what I believe is believable because damn it.

Praise the Lord!

I believe that guys that like girls are called girly men, but what about guys that like to hang around other guys, what do you call them? Penis men.

I believe that curiosity can lead to interesting places.

Hmmm.

I believe married men that go to bars to pick up women are called womanizers, but what about women that go to bars to pick up women what are they called? Women nicer.

Good God.

I believe that if things are not going your way, then follow the things.

Get it.

I believe if things are not going your way, tell things which way you want to go.

I believe that when you were younger, you would have fits of hunger and you would eat. Now that you are an adult, if you get fits of hunger, you would starve because you don't want to gain weight.

The Great Freddy Velez

Jacka———!

I believe that if things are not going your way, turn around.

I believe that the Seine do as I say not what I do is full of hole in a lot of ass-kicking going against you.

There's nobody out there that loves the sound of snow falling more than I do.

Get it?

I believe that if you want your kitchen to look bigger, lose weight.

Easy.

I believe that if you believe in love, then why not spread it like wildfire?

Good thinking.

I believe that if you are as smart as you say, then why not put your brain to good use.

I believe if you are all alone, you will pay. If you owe a favor, you will pay. But if they owe you a loan and a favor, you will wait and wait and wait.

I believe if things are not going your way, tell things which way you want to go.

Ain't that something?

I Might Be Wrong, but I'm Not

I believe that if you want to have your life, add music. Happier day, add music. A romantic evening, add music. Time alone, add music. Music is like the color white. It goes with everything.

Believe that.

I believe that if you want or would like to change, start with yourself.

Believe that.

I believe that if you want to be the master, you will have to share some of what you know. How are we to know if the master won't share?

Jacka———!

I believe that if the love of your life has left you for somebody else, then you need to get a pet like a rat.

Go figure.

I believe that if you are looking for love and can't find any, then you are either not good-looking in the right places or your credentials are not good.

Lord, have mercy.

I believe that if you want to be in the spotlight, standing in front of a semi, doing sixty at nighttime.

You're on!

I believe that you can find love and do what you love best, nothing.

The Great Freddy Velez

I believe that James plays an important part in everyday life.

Keep dreaming.

I believe that if you hate traffic, you shouldn't drive.

Jacka———!

I believe that everybody can be productive, even if it's just getting water for the ones doing the work.

I believe that you should use the pros and cons when considering something new.

I believe in a woman who is five feet ten in tall 150 pounds. I guess you could say that she is built better and more solid than a military latrine.

No lie.

I believe that we still have women meaner than a skunk on steroids in this world.

No lie.

I believe that there is not much difference between a dog in heat and a woman in heat. The dog will live with her tail and find her boy, and a woman will go to a bar and find her dog.

No kidding.

But the longer woman goes without a man, the meaner she gets.

No kidding.

I believe that a man in heat and broke will put his right hand or left hand to use.

No kidding.

How do I let a man who can go without a woman for one month is either thinking of suicide or turning gay?

Holy cow!

I believe money is good to have, but really, who needs it? I do.

Really.

I believe that I have the solution to get this world back on track. Here it is. Take a gay man that plays the part of a woman and take a lesbian woman that plays a part of the man and hook them up. Now you have a couple that could remain in the closet and nobody would know.

Hallelujah, brothers and sisters!

I believe that if a man is thinking about going gay, he should go to a doctor and get a prostate exam. If he likes how it feels, he was born to be a homo. If he doesn't like it, he was born to be a stud.

Praise the Lord!

Good human being starts at the heart. Being a son of a b—— begins as soon as you open your mouth.

Believe it or not.

I believe it if there is reincarnation, I want to come back as a fly.

The Great Freddy Velez

Believe it.

I believe that sex is bad. That is why the priestess and the nuns hide it.

You go, guys.

I believe that the next order of business for Congress is to pass a law that would prevent senior citizens from having sex and bringing their own grandchildren to this world.

Say that.

I believe you are a nobody if no one is saying anything about you behind your back.

Go figure.

I believe that you are not a good parent if your kid loves you all the time, even when you say no.

Go figure.

I believe that if you want to be a good parent, let your kids do whatever they want when they want. Just have bail money ready.

Go figure.

I believe that you should press just because you found out that you are not 100 percent of the nationality of your parents.

I believe that if you are a depressed person and are thinking of doing something stupid and you have money, think of the things I can do with your money when you are gone.

I Might Be Wrong, but I'm Not

Depressed no longer.

I believe that one on one is a couple, one onto was a good company, but what about three and four? I believe that would be seven.

There is a heaven.

Money away, they paid to have somebody put mud in their face while all they have to do is go outside, get some dirt and put water on it, and ta-da.

Same results.

I believe that you don't have to be depressed to feel depressed. For example, if you are used to seeing a $500 check every week but now you are working at McDonald's, your check is $150. You are going to be depressed until your next Happy Meal.

Ta-da!

I believe that when you are 150 pounds overweight, even your own belly doesn't want to be seen with you. You walk straight, and your belly is going side to side so nobody sees you together.

That's a shame.

I believe that if you want to pick up some good jokes, you go to the house of Congress. You can either listen to the jokes and see them in person for the price of one.

House of jokers.

The Great Freddy Velez

I believe that when Ronald Reagan left office, he took his Oscar with him. There are no more actors that can play the part of a politician like he did.

I believe that three-quarters of the voting public has lost trust in our government.

Me too.

I believe that we have too many lawyers in Washington and none of them have character. Lawyers should be utilized as advisers only, not lawmakers. Let the voters make the laws.

Jacka———!

I believe that everybody is always wondering when that day is coming but is always praying that it wouldn't be today.

Praise the Lord!

I believe that when that day comes, you would not even know what day it was or even care what day it was.

Good lord!

I believe that when that day comes, you would not be able to read it in the newspaper because you would not get the paper that day. You'll be out of town—oops, I mean I have this world.

Praise the Lord!

I believe that when you have energy, all you need to do is make it happen.

I Might Be Wrong, but I'm Not

Believe.

I believe that if you got all the pieces of the puzzle, then put it together. Time is money.

Move.

I believe that if you relax, you can figure it out.

Really.

I believe that sometimes what you thought would not work turns out better than you thought.

Believe it.

Fall in your lap and accept it as a gift.

I believe that everybody loves a little action in their lives, but you also need a little stability.

I believe everyone should watch out for surprises.

I believe that if you show interest, it will make everything more interesting.

Believe it.

I believe that when you are poor, you don't worry about anybody stealing your money, but they have a problem with trying to steal their food.

Oh sh——t!

The Great Freddy Velez

I believe that when you have money, you don't worry about people stealing your food, but you would take a life if they mess with your money.

Believe it or not.

I believe that the more you learn about relationships around you, the more you fall in love with your spouse.

I believe a good starting point is with the truth.

Believe it or not.

I believe that everybody should learn how to talk less and listen more and learn how to digest the conversation or whatever it is going on.

Trust me.

I believe people should focus on the openings, not the roadblocks. Think outside the box.

Jacka——es!

I believe that if you just focus, focus, focus, and forget about your surroundings, you are going to get screwed.

Believe it.

I believe that if you are screwing around, not paying attention to your surroundings, and not focusing, you are not only going to get screwed. You're going to get f——gered.

Jacka——!

I believe that the best gift you can give your better half is quality time.

Believe that.

I believe that there is nothing wrong with getting romantic more than once a day. As long as it is with the same partner.

Yeah, baby!

I believe you should not let out all your emotions in one sitting. Save some for a rainy day.

I believe that if happiness is a warm little p——ssy, then everybody should adopt a kitty.

Goodness gracious!

I believe that if there is a full moon and you hear howling, it could be your mother-in-law.

Praise the Lord.

I believe that if you don't want to watch what you eat, take off your glasses.

Hallelujah!

I believe the majority of the married population wants to be parents until it is time to clean the baby.

Oh god!

The Great Freddy Velez

I believe the reason a baby's poop stinks up the house so easily is because they spend nine months holding it in.

Take that to the bank.

I believe it is an injustice that a baby cannot eat solid food until he or she is six months old while his or her mother ate all kinds of garbage that he or she didn't like when they were in their bellies.

Go figure.

I believe that if you believe in what I believe in, then you are unbelievable. I sometimes don't believe in things I believe are believable because I don't think it is believable to leave.

Got that?

I believe God created woman, and I believe I created four. I'm winning.

I believe God created man.

Whopee-doo!

I believe God created ugly people just to keep children in place.

I believe God created beautiful people so they can look at the ugly people and tell them how beautiful they are.

Yeah right.

I believe God created bad people just to keep us on our toes.

Trust no one.

I believe when God said, "Who wants to be a millionaire?" I wasn't listening. I was looking at Halle Berry.

B———tch!

I believe in God said who wants to be a b———tch, I raised my hand. I thought he said who wants to go to the beach.

Hearing aid time.

I believe in the good and the bad and the ugly. You do ugly things that are good and bad when you are naked.

Believe it or not.

It's not really good or really bad or ugly—it's human nature.

I believe it is not really so bad to spend time alone in the bedroom with a *Playboy* magazine or a *Hustler*. It makes good reading. Only bad thing about it is you get calluses on your hand holding the book.

Oh man!

I believe I got the weirdest heroes: Hugh Hefner, Larry Flynn, and Mickey Rooney. I like this guy because they like to share love.

God bless them.

I believe women change with the times. I remember when I was seven years old, teenage girls used to hug me and kiss me. Now that I'm a man, they don't remember those days.

The Great Freddy Velez

Go figure.

I believe in what I am because I am what I am and I am that's it.

I am.

I believe a woman can have a man on the first date, depending on what she's got to offer and if she can cook.

Yeah, Mama!

I believe any woman that can cook will find a good man.

Oh yeah.

I believe it was God who said that thou shalt not commit adultery. That's because the Lord has never seen Halle Berry naked. If He did, He would say, "O God." He will call the Father and the Holy Spirit, and they will say, "Let us pray."

I believe Saddam Hussein's last words were "Oh sh———t."

I believe in changing of the guard. After eight hours, you need changing.

Gotcha, didn't I?

I believe that if it smells like roadkill, it must be collard greens.

I believe that if it smells like Lemon Pledge, it must be my wife coming in the door.

I believe if it looks like a man but walks like a woman, then it must be a cop.

I believe that if it looks like a priest but talks I can't judge, it means to kiss your ass goodbye for a while.

Mercy!

I believe that if she looks like a nun and smiles Mistress Li at you, it only means that she wants to leave the car or wants a bottle of wine or both.

Oh, God, forgive me.

I believe that if he smells like a drunk, he probably is, and if she smells like a drunk, she was probably kissing him.

I believe I live for the moment, so, Halle, your moment has arrived. Don't make me beg for my moment. Okay, I'll beg. Please.

I believe the *Mona Lisa* smile is just like my wife's until they open their mouths. Then time to move on to the liquor cabinet.

Good Lord!

I believe in a nice foot-long cigar after six. Just don't let my wife see it. She'll probably trade me for the cigar.

Probably.

I believe that the first time is very special. That rice and beans were out of this world.

Gotcha!

I believe that just because one is red and the other one is dark red, it doesn't mean it is an apple in the tomato—it could mean somebody kicked you in the groin. If it hurts, that's what it was.

The Great Freddy Velez

Ouch!

I believe deep in my heart that you don't need to fall flat on your face to feel pain. You don't need anybody to hit you either. Love will do this without even trying.

Love is painful.

I believe the last time I felt pain for love was when I hit my thumb with a hammer. Oh god, I love that thumb! He was my favorite.

I believe too much of a good thing is not good for anybody. That's why I keep telling my wife that if she wants to leave, she can. I'm too much of a good thing.

Liar.

I believe the only time too much of a good thing is not good for you is when you are having a good time.

You figure it out.

I believe that the Lord didn't put brothers and sisters in this world to kill each other over a can of soda, slice of pizza, or for using too much bathroom toilet paper. Go figure.

Lord, have mercy on my soul.

I believe I know more about the future than people give me credit for. I don't think the future could be any worse than what the world is going through right now.

I Might Be Wrong, but I'm Not

I believe with Bin Laden, Hussein, and Kadhafi out of the picture the world, democracy is looking better. Just two to go, Castro and Chavez. What a wonderful world this will be.

Hallelujah!

Praise the Lord!

I believe tension brings out the best in people.

I believe kiss houses were asked Jesus never accomplish their potential unless ass-kissing with their accomplishment.

Good lord!

I believed I could until my wife told me differently.

I believe you let people know about you, the harder you are to figure out. The harder you are to figure out, the more people want to know about you.

I believe you do a lot of stupid things as a kid. I guess time has a way of knocking the stupid out of you.

Praise the Lord!

I believe in the golden years. The golden years are when you are having fun and everything smells like a rose. The dark years are when you have to take orders because you are locked up. The ugly years are when you are having a little problem making ends meet, but it is better than being locked up.

Praise the Lord!

The Great Freddy Velez

I believe in the saying, don't knock it till you try it. Don't judge a book by its cover. Don't go by looks. Looks can be deceiving. I believe in all of them. If you taste it, you can criticize. If you read it, you can criticize. If you talk to him or her you can criticize. Until then, shut up.

Praise the Lord!

I believe in what the second-grader told me when I was growing up. He said, if you are going to be a dishwasher, be the best dishwasher in the world. If you're going to be a garbage man, be the best garbage man in the world. If you ever run for office, any kind, make sure you are doing it to help your fellow man, not your ego. These words are spoken to me by the smartest man in the world. My father.

God bless the man.

I believe that if you believe everything people tell you that not only are you a fool but a jackass at that. Fool.

I believe that if a man or woman tells you they love you, but you're not coming to a coffee shop to meet you, it is because they are either married or just want a good time. Stay back, way back, Facebook is a b——tch.

I believe having children makes you smarter. Once you have them, you wish you would have waited.

I believe that proper rest, a clear conscience, and a good haircut can get you inside the door. The rest is up to you to impress.

I believe that if you have the looks, the goods, but don't know how to present them, you have nothing.

Praise the Lord!

I believe that if you express yourself clearly and with good effective communication, you'll reach your goal.

I believe that in order to be accepted, you have to be a good listener or an ass-kisser or both.

Good God.

I believe in a simple life—staying single.

I believe if you want a challenging life, get married and bring that your in-laws to live with you.

Now that's a challenge.

Lord, have mercy.

I believe if you want everything in your life positive, stay away from liquor, drugs, and women.

You sissy. God bless!

I believe that the smarter people get in this world, the less violence there is.

Praise the Lord!

I believe you can call the Republicans or the Democrats to animals on the endangered species list.

I believe that you can kill your own dream by believing a politician smith. You will never own anything following a politician's theories.

The Great Freddy Velez

Good lord!

I believe daydreaming is bad for day driving—you just missed your exit.

Good God Almighty!

I believe I am the coolest man under pressure. My wife could be kissing my neck, blowing in my ear, and I became stiff. Get it? Stiff under pressure.

Good God Almighty!

I believe winners don't always finish first. Sometimes coming last has its benefits. The winner gets to drink all the Jack Daniel's he wants. The loser gets to take the girl home.

Good God, yeah, baby!

I believe in the winning loser, that's a man that gets to pick first in a contest of one hundred women when he picks a transvestite.

Holy sh——t!

I believe the winning loser when it comes to women is a woman who picks first on one hundred men, and she picks the one that doesn't like women.

Holy Mother of God!

I believe you picked the right one, like me because my wife says so.

Amen to that.

I believe that if you tell them the truth and they don't like it, you did a wonderful job.

I believe that if you can't handle the truth, get over it. Move on.

I believe that I am not going to stay gorgeous forever, so, Halle, get it. Move on.

Please.

I believe that if you don't take risks, you will never know whether you are going to make it or not. Go for it.

I believe that paying attention to little details can make work or playing easier.

I believe in biting more than I can chew. That way, I know what I can handle or not. You'll surprise yourself with what you can do.

Praise the Lord!

I believe in the imagination game. You make up the rules. Oh, Halle. Use imagination properly.

Good God.

I believe staying in a good mood makes everybody around you, and the day goes smoother and happier.

I believe that if you are that person that gets invited to even a garage sale, you have it. You may not even know that you have it. Don't change.

Hallelujah!

The Great Freddy Velez

I believe you don't have to be married to have a connection, just a good mindset.

I believe that it doesn't matter how many times you ring the doorbell or knock on the door. If they don't open, that means you are not welcomed. Get the hint.

Bye!

I believe that if a woman asks you if those pants make her look big, be honest and tell her no. Your big ass makes those pants look big.

Hallelujah!

I believe that if a woman asks you if anything she wears makes her look big, tell her what she wants to hear, no. Honey, you will be a happy camper.

I believe anybody can move a mountain if they are persistent enough to move one piece of rock at a time.

Be persistent.

I believe that if you are confident and are sure of yourself, make sure you don't cross somebody else's territory or hurt their feelings.

Don't be too cocky.

I believe that people learn how to live once they have hit some humps and lumps and have fallen on their faces at least once.

I believe that if you feel happy about your decision, no explanation is needed.

Have faith.

I believe I am the greatest dad of all time. After all, I do as my kids say.

I think is what.

I believe I am the greatest husband too. I do as I'm told.

Good grief!

I believe everybody can make a difference in this world if they only knew how little of their time was needed. You can make a difference just by holding somebody's hand or opening a door, or volunteering time, or just being there.

I believe God gave grandchildren to some people to extend their lives so he can show them what they put their parents through growing up.

Oh my God!

I believe when you have grown grandkids, they act more like the grandparent and the grandparent like kids.

Go figure.

I believe grandkids are a blessing in disguise of yourself when young.

Believe it or not.

The Great Freddy Velez

I believe you will not leave this war of them to pay for what you have done wrong.

Oh my god!

I believe there is no do-over.

Lord have mercy on my a———!

I believe you are a person of your word if you can keep the word to yourself. When you say that you were going to do something good for yourself like lose weight, stop smoking, or eating right,

Then I'll believe.

I believe that a lot of Christians are not as Christian as they think. A Christian is not constantly criticizing what others wear or eat, or who their friends are, or where they hang out, or how they make their money. I don't think you should call yourself a Christian if you do any of these things.

My God with you, Christians!

I believe the Lord gave everybody a tongue to do as they please, except to criticize negatively.

Christian, my a———!

I believe that if you are going to criticize, look into your surrounding areas and family history before you do.

Christian.

I believe that not even the pope can criticize anyone for farting 'cause I am sure he has.

Praise the Lord!

I believe you are as good as you think you are or people say you are.

Think about it.

I believe that I was put in this world to be a gigolo. It's just that it's not working out that way.

Damn!

I believe my wife calls me a gigolo or did she say "G, go low?"

Same sh——t.

I believe that you don't have to be an all-out Christian to have been blessed with good fortune. I've been blessed far more than I expected. If you have faith in the Lord, the Lord will bless you.

If you sneeze, the Lord will bless you.

I believe and have faith.

I believe that if you enjoy lying to people, you should be a politician. If you don't agree with anything others have to say, then you belong in the house of Congress. You're a true poop.

I believe with everything happening around the world—earthquakes, hurricanes, tsunamis. I think this is God's way of letting you know that he is tired of all the bickering.

I believe that 90 percent of the politicians in office are lawyers. Is it because they know the law? Or is it because they want to help their fellow men? In any case, they can all bite me.

The Great Freddy Velez

I believe everybody can have a friend like I do—loyal, trustworthy, great with kids, brave, and a joy to be around. He is my dog. I just call him Muhammad Ali because he is the greatest. My wife has a little Trump—oh, that she calls a b———.

I believe that if you believe in psychics, you are a fool. Don't need your money for a good cause, not a thief.

Jacka———!

I believe that if a psychic could read your mind, they would be working in law enforcement.

More than half of the population in the world would be in jail.

I believe there is not much difference between a hoarder and a slob.

I believe that when you say nobody understands me but your mother says I understand you, that is even worse.

Lord, have mercy.

I believe it was my wife who said to me you and your dog have a lot in common—food and sex.

What a life!

I believe that if somebody is slaving and pushing you, you should try to get close to a door, so on the next push, you can run.

Good thinking.

I believe that if you speak loud and clear, you don't have to rely on somebody else doing somebody else's job.

I Might Be Wrong, but I'm Not

Speak up.

I believe that if you grew up being a mama's boy, you are in a lot of trouble when you get married. Wifey doesn't play those games.

Oh sh——t!

I believe the future looks better than the present. I also know that I'm lying to myself.

I believe that if you want your woman to join the gym, just show her Victoria's Secret catalog.

She'll be there tomorrow.

There is heaven.

I believe nobody has the right to make the American people suffer needlessly—oops, sorry about that Congress does.

Jacka——es!

I believe that if you are a real down-to-earth human being, you will believe in Santa, the tooth fairy, but not in the people running our country.

Jacka——es!

I believe that if you live paycheck to paycheck, you should eat every other day to stay afloat.

Bills must be paid before you feed your family. You know that.
Thanks Uncle Sam!

The Great Freddy Velez

I believe that if you stand on an Echo Mountain and scream hello out there and their reply is "Forget about it," it is time to move on.

Creepy.

I believe in apple pie and whipped cream.

Oh yeah!

I believe everybody wishes they could make everybody happy, safe, comfortable, unprotected all the time, but it's impossible.

Not all the time.

I believe that it is better to better yourself than being the cool one. Want a better life? Being cool isn't going to get you there.

Get it.

I believe you can make your own excitement in your life. All you need is a little change here and there.

So there.

I believe happiness is winning an argument over your know-it-all spouse.

I believe men use only 90 percent of their brains: 45 percent sports, 45 percent sex, and the rest is just waste.

Believe it or not.

I believe that you should commit to what makes you happy, not what some other person recommends.

Be yourself.

I believe that if you reduce your needs, life will be simpler and more enjoyable.

I believe it if you show fear, it will never get done. Don't let fear stop your dreams.

Believe.

I believe that if you use your memory right, you can make tons of money. Remember those dreams. Never lose hope.

Believe.

I believe everybody has a three-eighth of mind to make something beautiful out of what some others called garbage.

I believe that if you have good intentions, it will happen. Just give yourself that little push.

I believe you should never change your stance on an issue just because somebody asks you to. You know your mind better than anybody.

Stand firm.

I believe that if you see somebody doing something good for somebody, this inspires you to do the same. This will expand your vision to make this a better world to live in.

I believe that if you have a good heart and mind, you can like the life of the less fortunate.

Praise the Lord!

The Great Freddy Velez

I believe it if you want to challenge, take the more difficult one and an impossible one to do.

Try it. You will like it.

I believe that if you are simply not yourself, take a break. The brain also needs a break once in a while.

I believe if you have a good heart, nothing can stop you from spreading sunshine at night time.

Hallelujah!

I believe I never heard the priest say anything about a choke collar on my neck.

Good lord!

I believe that the only office I am running to is my office, the bathroom.

Take that.

I believe that if you want to be a candidate for office in the Washington, DC, area, make sure you have paid off all your skeletons in the closet. All the boobs in Washington, DC, and none have ever done anything wrong. Just lie.

I'm innocent.

I believe that if Washington is trying to cut weight, they should start at the porta-potty in Congress. It's beginning to smell bad.

Really bad.

I believe that I don't understand who the real prisoners are in my country, the bad people in jail, or the good hardworking people not in jail who have to pay for those in jail.

Hard to believe.

I believe tips for Tots are not fair for a man that enjoys a glass of milk once in a while.

I believe that the saying goes, the voters get their chance to speak. That translates to just bones shut up. We (Congress) got this.

Believe it or not.

I believe that unless you have been homeless or gone hungry for days, you can't say I know what you are going through. You don't really know what the experience is like until you've actually been there.

I believe it is stupid to argue about religion, especially when they all believe in God, both different translations. God has many names got that?

Jesus Christ.

I believe that if you say I am in love with my God, then you are an amazing human being.

Never change.

I believe that if you think greed is good, then you go to the ballpark and pay $10 for a hot dog and $12 for a beer and leave your kids at home. Don't forget the autograph.

The Great Freddy Velez

Jacka——! Unbelievable

I believe, really believe, that you can speed it up if you really, really want to.

Oh God!

I believe in all honesty that stupidity comes in all shapes, nationalities, colors, sexes, etc., etc., etc., even in animals.

Good lord!

I believe that the best surprises are the ones made at the moment, especially for kids.

I believe that anybody has a sense of how to make money, but they don't have money to make sense.

Go figure.

I believe everyone has something to teach anyone who will listen.

Believe it or not.

I believe that if you know nature, you would dress accordingly, you would not wear a coat in July, and he would not go to the beach and a G-string in New York in December.

Jacka——!

I believe that if you have a lot of knowledge of something, sometimes it is not good to show it.

You will get screwed.

I Might Be Wrong, but I'm Not

Believe it or not.

I believe that if you keep your message short, people remember more than the priests the sermon.

Believe it.

I believe that if you have a nice personality, people will notice immediately even if you're fat.

Yeah, baby.

I believe that 90 percent of men are weak when it comes to women. A woman knows when she has him in her pocket.

Believe it.

I believe everybody is going to be eighteen for only 365 or 6 days once.

Enjoy!

I believe if you know what makes you happy, keep doing it.

Praise the Lord!

I believe people are amazing, especially when they don't bother you.

I believe that certain secrets are to be kept to yourself. Telling someone your secrets can come back and bite you in the butt.

Honestly.

The Great Freddy Velez

I believe that if someone wants to know your secret, it is because that person wants to have something on you for his or her future.

Mouth shut keeps the flies away.

I believe that if a friend has made a difference in your life, you should try to make a difference in somebody else's too, even if it is a stranger.

I believe that I don't recognize myself in the mirror in the mornings. I wonder if it has something to do with the makeup or the wig.

I believe Congress works for the people of other countries. They spend millions of dollars on other countries. They rebuild countries with our money. Something doesn't sound right. Where is the "united we stand"?

I believe that all politicians have the talent and experience to fool all the people all the time. They promised this and promised, and then they say to the world, "Fooled you, didn't I?"

Reelect this man.

I believe the way things are going: the filthy rich will become just millionaires, the millionaires will become middle class, the middle class will become poor, and the poor will become the third world.

Believe it or not.

More and more people are eating leftovers than ever before. Repeat that the food was that good, or that food is getting more expensive to go to waste.

I believe that if Congress is supposed to be working for us then why are we not moving on up. Instead, we are moving on down, losing jobs overseas, losing our homes, losing our soldiers to unnecessary wars.

What gives?

I believe that if you fool me once, that's okay. Fool me twice, well, that's okay too, but fool me three times, damn, you are good.

Congress.

I believe that if you don't value what you have, eventually, you will lose it. It may be family, job, or material things.

Value what you have.

I believe that being supportive is better than talking. You don't need anybody talking and not being supportive.

Support, don't talk.

I believe that I've been doing this for years, taking me nuts to bed with me.

Two nuts, get it?

I believe that when things are good, we don't realize how fortunate we are to have it all while others just wonder what it's like.

I believe I cannot take my dog to the psychiatrist. He only allows humans on his couch. Get it?

I believe it is time we start celebrating ourselves.

The Great Freddy Velez

Yeah, baby.

I believe life is unpredictable, so take every day as it comes. Make the best of it.

I believe that people fall in love when they are unconscious. Otherwise, there wouldn't be so many divorces.

I believe you don't see your mistakes like others see them. Sometimes they have to be brought to your attention.

That's what friends are for.

I believe nothing has ever changed just by wishing. Wishing has nothing to do with change.

Take charge.

I believe that if you have never been embarrassed, you don't know what life is all about.

I believe that if a person says that they have never been embarrassed, they are the biggest liars of all time.

I believe that if you have an interest in anything, follow through.

Believe.

I believe everybody at one time or another has said I've been there and done that.

I believe it if you really want to remember something, you will write it down.

But if you don't make the first move, you will never know if the connection is there.

Go for it.

I believe in avoiding smooth talkers, they will always get you.

I believe that if you challenge yourself, you'll feel better on the inside. No challenge, no guts.

I believe that the imagination is a hell of a tool.

Imagine that.

I believe if you want to feel great about yourself, inspire others to use their imagination and challenges said they didn't know they had thought of.

Little help.

I believe that if you are forty, but she is like an eighty-year-old, then you are old. You are eighty but feel like a forty-year-old, then you are young at heart. It's all mental.

Hallelujah!

I believe that our country has more jobs for the American people than they realize. It's just that they are all overseas.

Good gracious!

I believe that if you walk into a room and it smells really bad, it can only mean that there are politicians working in the room looking for votes.

The Great Freddy Velez

I believe that children that misbehave anywhere they go learn this at home. Poor parenting.

I believe that if you teach your kids that lying, bullying, stealing, cheating, or disrespecting the elderly will not be tolerated in your household, they will learn that life could be beautiful without all the nonsense.

I believe the best gift you can give anybody is your time. They will feel the love.

I believe that if you are an optimistic upbeat person, then you are brilliant even if you dress.

Funny.

I believe things don't have to happen to you for you to feel the hurt. I guess if you don't feel anything, you don't have a heart.

I believe that just because your hair is turning gray or white doesn't mean you're getting old.

Gray or white means maturity.

I believe in a woman that's good-looking is okay, but a woman that knows how to cook is drop-dead gorgeous.

Oh yeah, baby!

I believe that it is only in the movies where the guy meets the girl and in the next scene, they're in bed. Regular people only get the last track on the first and last scene.

I believe you don't have to be a business genius to smell when something doesn't smell right.

I believe that the only people that you can let go about politics, religion, women, men are in the barbershop or beauty salon. Everybody loves to agree to disagree.

Get your stress out.

I believe that if you are feeling sorry for yourself while doing self-pity, then you need a garlic and onion sandwich.

Guarantee pick-me-up.

I believe that you should never put off what you can do today until tomorrow because tomorrow never comes. Just ask your spouse.

I believe that everybody is in this world for a reason. Just don't ask me what's the reason 'cause I don't know and don't care. I am just having fun while I still can.

I believe in love. I do. I really, really do. For real, I believe in love.

I believe I never really understand what love/hate relationships were until now. My wife loves me when she gets her way, but she hates me when I say no. What happens and what gives to fifty-fifty.

Love stinks.

I believe that I'm fascinating to someone I just don't know. I guess it's me. That's good enough.

I believe that in many ways I have blossomed, I'm more focused on my eating habits, and I organize my food so I can reach it safely without dropping it.

The Great Freddy Velez

Focus.

I believe that if I take a different action, I will probably get difficult results. Don't change what is working for you.

I believe that I have not lost my touch. It's just that I have to work on being more grateful to maintain it.

I believe that I am the safety net for my family, friends, enemies, and animals, and who knows what else.

I believe it if you want to have your weekends free, don't get married.

I believe that if you want to have your weekends free, cover all your activities and desires by Friday.

I believe that whatever you are hoping to gain by your efforts, might surprise you.

Work at it.

I believe that the saying goes, no pain, no gain, well, my friends, that's b———. I ate a twelve-inch sub, and there was no pain, but I gained.

I believe everybody has talent. It's just that you have to be at the right place at the right time and be able to kiss a little ass. Your talent might be just that, kiss-ass.

I believe that if you want to keep your favorite people around, communications work wonders.

Reach out, be there.

I believe rice and beans work wonders on an empty stomach.

I believe that there is always a question on everybody's mind. I deserve better, or I should be doing better. Gets? We as humans are never satisfied with what we got—we want more. Only animals are satisfied with what they got or have.

I believe that instead of bitching, do something about it. Move it.

Jacka——!

I believe that if the circumstances don't make you tense, then go for it. Add life to your day.

I believe with the way the world is now, even sitting around doing nothing is a risk.

I believe that the way things are going in this world, just thinking about something illegal can get you jail time or the gas chamber for that matter.

I believe that I am not a pedophile just because I think of Halle Berry in a G-string.

Oh God!

I believe that if you don't want to go to jail or prison, don't do anything that you know is an illegal jackass.

I believe that sitting around doing nothing for a day or two was a good healing process for the body and brain.

Relax.

The Great Freddy Velez

I believe that I honestly don't know who smells worse—the poops in Congress or a porta-potty.

Just about even.

I believe that fear only exists in the mind of the week, in sports. In real life, fear is a serious situation. It can make you do stupid things that actually didn't exist.

I believe that sometimes something small can make a big difference.

Yes, I do.

I believe that sometimes, no matter how dumb you are, just by keeping your mouth shut, you will look smart.

Go figure.

I believe that Christmas is a time to share and give to those less fortunate, not yourself.

A Lamborghini.

I believe you should not let the family know what they are getting once you die. You might die sooner than expected. Believe it.

Greed.

I believe sometimes you have to sit down and write the reasons why you are thankful. I personally am thankful that my children didn't follow in my footsteps. Well, two daughters are mean but beautiful.

I am thankful.

I believe that I am personally and thankful for the Halle Berry the Lord gave me. The best there is.

My wife.

I believe that women believe that by coloring their hair, their age will not go up. Well, ladies, wrong. Now will cost you more to look young.

That's all.

I believe that sometimes your confidence or brain plays tricks with you, the one you feel uncertain, don't let anybody see it.

Power through.

I believe that even adults say we are there yet.

Believe it or not.

I believe that every action you take, you are the only one that knows whether it was a success or not.

I believe that you are the only person that can determine how you can feel at any given time.

Doctors can't do that.

I believe you can focus on the more important issues. Eliminate the fact.

The Great Freddy Velez

Get it?

I believe that if the sign says Help Wanted, ask, "Help for what?" especially if the sign is in a manure shop.

Got it? Sh——t!

I believe that if you are a team or a couple where everything is supposed to be fifty-fifty but everything you do is either wrong or gets negative feedback and you still try to do things their way and it is still getting negative feedback, well, my friend, it is time to move on. There's something good or better just around the corner.

Move on.

I believe that just because you don't care what is going on around you or in the world doesn't mean you have attention deficit disorder. It only means that you want to live your life the way you want to live it—no obstacles.

I believe that if a person is getting attention deficit disorder drugs and is still not paying attention, then bring on the big guns, Puerto Rican rice, and beans.

Disorder restored.

I believe everybody should enjoy life on their own terms. Don't let anyone dictate your terms for a good life.

Enjoy what you want.

I believe that we live in an era that requires everybody to set a new standard to live a normal life.

Believe it or not.

I Might Be Wrong, but I'm Not

The way that everybody should enjoy life, family, friends, and a little time they got left in this world. Before you realize you are too old to do anything that could have been done years ago.

Life is short. Enjoy it.

I believe that if you have friends of different races, religions, political parties, and you are having a get-together before anything starts, let them know which topics turn off the table. I believe everybody has an opinion on everything and that they're always right. Avoid hurting feelings.

I drink to that.

I believe that even the most honest person lies just to not hurt somebody's feelings.

I believe that our people never find something beautiful in anybody, even if they know that it looks good.

I believe that if you get offended easily, don't open your mouth unless it is to put food in it.

I believe that if a person says I'm a wonderful human being, they're lying. You let others say that.

Not yourself.

I believe if a person says that they're not mean-spirited, they are lying. They're meaner than a pit bull with rabies.

I believe you never ask your spouse "What did I do wrong?" you are going to get more than you're bargaining for. Things that you don't even remember.

The Great Freddy Velez

I believe that people that donate big bucks at a political party checking something in return.

Go figure.

I believe that you could say that we live in a different world today.

It's called a material world.

I believe for a long time that Black Friday was used only for the stock market.

I believe that you don't have to wait for Thanksgiving to eat turkey. People, it's just a tradition. There's nothing wrong with turkey and rice and beans every Saturday or Sunday and nauseous on Thursday once a year.

I believe that she wanted to spend her husband's money or anything that looks good on her.

Oh God!

I believe most men like it when the time goes back an hour it means their wife can't spend all their hard-earned money in one day.

I believe that sometimes that location, career, and relationships are not as perfect as you think.

Feel nauseous yet?

I believe it sometimes you have to take a break, sit down, and analyze how to improve and manage your life. It's not all working money. You have a life.

I Might Be Wrong, but I'm Not

Think.

I believe you can think better with a full stomach.

You are a sharp dresser and have a good appearance even if you are broke. People talk good things, even copy you.

Believe it or not.

I believe that if you want to be your own boss, you have to take the first step. Make sure before that first step that the ground is hard because there will be some roadblocks and Thompson lumps.

Don't lose hope.

I believe that the more you accept yourself the way you are the less questions you need to ask others.

I believe that if you are having an argument in your mind, there are no losers or winners.

Nobody hurts.

I wonder if you look at your past and you will find that you have come a long way.

Praise the Lord!

I believe expensive shoes don't make a man.

I believe that if you are happy with your appearance, then let them talk.

Yeah, baby.

The Great Freddy Velez

If you have confidence, you can override any situation regardless of your preparation on the matter at hand.

I believe people or everybody needs positive people around them that provide energy and emotional support when you are down.

I believe that the only place that your plans are always correct with no mistakes is in your brain. I believe you are not living life if everything is routine. Change that routine and live life.

I believe not everybody is going to believe in your acts or beliefs.

Ignore them.

I believe that if you got that fire inside you but don't know what to do, then go take a shower.

I believe that a conservative is really an elephant just like a jackass.

Praise the Lord!

I believe that if crossing a border to better family life is criminal, then half of the United States should be in jail. How many 100 percent Americans do we have in our country? The federal government should go after real criminals, not those who want to feed a family. Not all immigrants are bad. We have our old apple. We have bad apples at Steeler robbery immigrants, and some of these apples work for the federal government.

Live and let live.

I believe that if you take a sniff and it smells bad, then it must be bad. It's not necessarily garbage. Only it could be a bad apple coming your way.

The nose never lies.

I believe that if it tastes bad or smells better but looks bad, then it must be bad.

Jacka———!

Good lord!

I believe that if you are committed to do the right thing, it doesn't matter where you come from. You will succeed.

Believe.

I believe that the music of the fifties, sixties, and seventies will never come back but will never be forgotten.

Take that to the bank.

I believe everybody's skills start with a good conversation. A good conversation will start your imagination beyond your control.

Imagine that.

I believe that what you thought was unreachable is now much easier to accomplish.

Believe.

I believe you can impress those that are difficult to impress if you got the "it."

The Great Freddy Velez

Believe it.

I believe you should take risks to get what you want. A little risk could be worthwhile.

Believe.

I believe you should never show to see in your face.

I believe that if you maintain a solid stance, you'll become more believable. Keep a solid stance even if everything inside your body is shaking. You win.

Yeah, baby.

I believe a little creativity will accomplish where others fail.

I believe you should be loud enough just to show how thrilling and enthusiastic you are. Don't go overboard. It will show.

I believe that when it comes to family, distance should not be a factor. Making a plan with detail should bring that gap closer.

Happiness.

I believe that we all want to see some qualities in people that even when we know they don't have it, we wish they did.

I believe the more that is kept on said, the more complicated the matter will get. Speak your mind without hurting feelings. Forget the feelings. Speak your mind.

Prevent an ulcer.

I believe that if you hang around somebody that is a bad influence, cruel, and nasty, you just want attention.

Jacka———!

I believe that when any of your children or grandchildren give you a smile for no reason, they're up to something. Brings back old memories.

I believe that when your child a grandchild gives you a smile for no reason, just ask, "Okay, what do you need or what do you want?"

I believe that if you are a hundred or more years old, you are here to teach those that they call senior citizens how to live on Social Security.

I believe that when you stay what you think out loud, it could be a risk. Write it down and stand back. Look to see who was around before opening your mouth.

I believe that everybody has a vivid imagination or picture of how they want to be or live.

I believe I reach my personal promised land.

I believe that if you got a clear head, you can adjust your actions before doing something stupid.

Think.

I believe that with the invention of Google, you don't need to spend thousands of dollars to travel to any country. You can go to any street corner or restaurant and see what's happening.

Google, Google.

The Great Freddy Velez

I believe it if you focus on what they put in front of you or who they put in front of you, you can see right through them.

Focus.

I believe that there are good things in store for those that keep their mouth shut.

I believe that if you concentrate you are not as tired as you think.

Concentrate.

I believe that if you concentrate on what you are doing, you will get done.

Willpower.

I believe everybody has five things that they can do to make this a better world. Number one, now let me see. Number two, now let me see. Number three, now let me see. Number four, now let me see. Number 5, now let me see. That's just about it. That let me see is not going to get done.

Well, just let me see.

Groundbreaking stuff.

I believe this nation is on a slow recovery. Are we talking about unemployment or sick people or both?

Both.

I believe that if you want the right answer, you talked to God. If you just want an answer whether it is right or wrong, you talk to Congress.

Lord, have mercy on those hoops.

I believe that we live in the land of the free. It's just that we cannot make our own decision on what is right or what is prohibited from us doing. The only thing free and not prohibited is breathing.

Good Lord!

I believe that if you want to know what is wrong in our country, ask the illegal people. They make more sense than those trying to run our nation.

I believe we as Americans have a lot to say on what we need to continue forward. Congress has the right to say shut up so they can continue doing nothing. For this, they get paid

Unbelievable.

I believe that as times go by, we have less and less to say on what's to be done to move ahead.

I believe that the best way to stay sane is to read the Bible or go crazy.

I believe my happiness comes from the Lord, my love comes from my Lord, and show peace comes from my Lord and grandchildren, and my joy comes from my Lord and those or anyone around me.

God is good.

The Great Freddy Velez

I believe you make your own happiness. Follow the truth.

I believe that there is no difference if you go to Hooters and wash girls with big boobs work or go to Washington and watch big boobs trying to run the country.

I love my country.

I believe that our country has bigger boobs than your country.

I believe unless you know somebody for at least ten years or more, this includes your spouse, you do not confess to anything.

Not guilty.

I believe that if you are in a good mood and feel like opening up before you open your mouth, it might end up full of flies.

Mouth shut, everybody happy.

I believe this world belongs to those who know what they want and are willing to do whatever it takes to get there. It's called hard work.

I believe this world belongs to those that believe that they belong.

I believe that if you are sincere and take your job seriously, chances are, you will be noticed by the right people. Pay no attention to those that work just for a paycheck.

Be yourself.

I believe that everybody at some time or another has had the common sense to kick them in the rear and made the right decision.

I believe that the pursuit of happiness is making the right decision.

I believe that just because you got perfect hair doesn't mean that makes you smart. A perfect body doesn't make you smart. Now a perfect body called perfect hair, and braves now you're cooking with gas.

Let's get it on.

I believe it's bad, really bad, to speculate how Halle Berry, Jennifer Lopez, Kim Kardashian, and Beyoncé soap up their bodies when showering. Oh god, speculation is alive and well.

Umm, God!

Long live speculation.

I believe that if you want to learn how to live, you have to accept people as they are and socialize with them.

Try it, you might like it.

I believe that if you are a good role model with a good heart, your siblings will be even better.

Believe it or not.

I believe it if you are making a once-in-a-lifetime decision, don't rush.

I believe it is easy to assemble a team if you are a friendly person. Everybody wants to be on your side.

The Great Freddy Velez

I believe it if you have an amazing attention span, you are really not listening. You are looking at the lady's breast.

Good lord!

I believe that if you come to a stop sign that says "Stop Thinking," it means just that. Pay attention.

Don't be thinking about what you want for dinner tonight.

I believe that if you have that great power of persuasion, you got it made and you don't know it.

Some people don't know how to use their powers positively.

I believe that everybody can be me. Whipple, no squeezing at the workplace, or the bathroom.

I believe the saying goes like this, money doesn't buy happiness. Well, that's a lie. It has brought me a lot.

Believe it or not.

I believe that the best part of the holiday is when they're over.

Believe it.

I believe you should think of an answer before speaking. My better half asked me if I ever wonder what would have happened if we never met. Well, I told her without thinking that I'll probably be rich and happy. Well, that couch is getting really comfortable.

Think.

I believe that the best time to start a diet is when your wife or husband is making turkey, tongue, and onion pepper casseroles.

Brrrr!

I believe that just because a person is tender-hearted doesn't mean he or she is not mentally and physically strong too. Obstacles, no problem.

I believe that if you want a makeover, what is stopping you? Be happy.

Be happy.

I believe that if your day starts wrong, you have the power to steer it in the right direction.

I believe that a difference of opinion is good for the soul.

I'll eat to that.

I believe that there is nothing wrong with being warm, patient, compassionate, and lovable.

Human.

I believe that when you are having fun, time flies.

I believe that when you are in a doctor's office or in jail time drags.

Go figure.

I believe you get more accomplished when you are a happy individual and love your surroundings.

The Great Freddy Velez

I believe that everybody recognizes when things are going right or their way.

I believe that everybody has the ability to make something that is not interesting interesting.

Yes, I do.

About the Author

Freddy has been married for forty-five years to his wife, Rosa. They have five children, sixteen grandchildren, and four great-grandchildren. He is originally from Asbury Park, New Jersey. Freddy currently lives in sunny Florida, enjoying his retirement. He is a Vietnam veteran who suffers from PTSD. Writing has helped him through the effects PTSD has on a person.